Proverbs 31 Woman

A TWELVE-WEEK STUDY GUIDE

AMANDA STONEMAN

TWS | THE WRITER'S SOCIETY PUBLISHING

To request permissions, contact TWS Publishing at www.thewriterssociety.online

Paperback: ISBN 978-1-961180-24-6

Scripture quotations marked TPT are from The Passion Translation®. Copyright © 2017, 2018, 2020 by Passion & Fire Ministries, Inc. Used by permission. All rights reserved. ThePassionTranslation.com.

TWS | The Writer's Society Publishing
Lodi, CA
www.thewriterssociety.online

To my husband Brian, our girls Katrina, Danielle, and Rachael! For their love and support through this whole process.

I would also like to extend my heartfelt gratitude to the Fredrickson and Hooper families!

Contents

Introduction

Welcome!

Thank you for participating in this study and the time to invest in yourself and your growth. In this 12-week study, you will discover who you are as the Proverbs 31 woman you were created to be. You will get the most out of this study by being honest and intentional with yourself as you progress through the materials.

When I first started reading and studying Proverbs 31 a few years back, I only focused on verses 10-31. I was immediately overwhelmed and stressed. How would I become this perfect woman who has it all together? This reaction started as I read verse 10, *"Who can find a virtuous wife..."* I thought: *well, I already failed, and I have not even started.* My understanding of the word virtuous was wrong. I thought it meant morally perfect, and I had made my share of mistakes in the past. Virtuous in this verse means strength, efficiency, and wealth, to name a few. Here is the link to see the meaning of virtuous (*chayil*): (HTTPS://BIBLEHUB.COM/HEBREW/2428.HTM) Learning and understanding this is life-changing!

INTRODUCTION

~ Amanda Stoneman

WELCOME VIDEO: HTTPS://YOUTU.BE/OKTQYSXNUKC

How to Use this Study Guide

Days 1 and 2: Read and Answer

On these days you will read the verse and then answer the thought-provoking questions.

Day 3: Video

Watch the video, read reading after the video and reread verses for the week. Take notes.

Day 4: Action Step and Prayer Tip

Do the action step and implement it and the prayer tip throughout the week.

Day 5: Highlights

Read the highlights and reflect. Also make your own highlights.

Days 6 and 7: Rest and Reflect

Now is the time to absorb all you have taken in Throughout the week. Take stock of and journal what you have learned.

Week 1: Perception

〜〜

DAY 1

[1] *King Lemuel's royal words of wisdom:*
These are the inspired words my mother taught me.
[2] *Listen, my dear son, son of my womb.*
You are the answer to my prayers, my son.
[3] *So keep yourself sexually pure*
from the promiscuous, wayward woman.
Don't waste the strength of your anointing
on those who ruin kings—
you'll live to regret it!
[4] *For you are a king, Lemuel,*
and it's never fitting for a king to be drunk on wine
or for rulers to crave alcohol.
[5] *For when they drink they forget justice*
and ignore the rights of those in need,
those who depend on them for leadership.
[6-7] *Strong drink is given to the terminally ill,*
who are suffering at the brink of death.
Wine is for those in depression
in order to drown their sorrows.

Let them drink and forget their poverty and misery.
⁸ But you are to be a king who speaks up on behalf
of the disenfranchised
and pleads for the legal rights of the defenseless
and those who are dying.
⁹ Be a righteous king, judging on behalf of the poor
and interceding for those most in need.

The Radiant Bride

¹⁰ Who could ever find a wife like this one —
she is a woman of strength and mighty valor!
She's full of wealth and wisdom.
The price paid for her was greater than many jewels.
¹¹ Her husband has entrusted his heart to her,
for she brings him the rich spoils of victory.
¹² All throughout her life she brings him what is good and not
*   evil.*
¹³ She searches out continually to possess
that which is pure and righteous.
She delights in the work of her hands.
¹⁴ She gives out revelation-truth to feed others.
She is like a trading ship bringing divine supplies
from the merchant.
¹⁵ Even in the night season she arises and sets food on the table
for hungry ones in her house and for others.
¹⁶ She sets her heart upon a field and takes it as her own.
She labors there to plant the living vines.
¹⁷ She wraps herself in strength, might, and power in all her
*   works.*
¹⁸ She tastes and experiences a better substance,
and her shining light will not be extinguished,
no matter how dark the night.
¹⁹ She stretches out her hands to help the needy

and she lays hold of the wheels of government.
20 She is known by her extravagant generosity to the poor,
for she always reaches out her hands to those in need.
21 She is not afraid of tribulation,
for all her household is covered in the dual garments
of righteousness and grace.
22 Her clothing is beautifully knit together —
a purple gown of exquisite linen.
23 Her husband is famous and admired by all,
sitting as the venerable judge of his people.
24 Even her works of righteousness
she does for the benefit of her enemies.
25 Bold power and glorious majesty are wrapped around her
as she laughs with joy over the latter days.
26 Her teachings are filled with wisdom and kindness
as loving instruction pours from her lips.
27 She watches over the ways of her household
and meets every need they have.
28 Her sons and daughters arise in one accord to extol her
virtues,
and her husband arises to speak of her in glowing terms.
29 "There are many valiant and noble ones,
but you have ascended above them all!"
30 Charm can be misleading,
and beauty is vain and so quickly fades,
but this virtuous woman lives in the wonder, awe,
and fear of the Lord.
She will be praised throughout eternity.
31 So go ahead and give her the credit that is due,
for she has become a radiant woman,
and all her loving works of righteousness deserve to be
admired
at the gateways of every city! (PROVERBS *31:1-31,* TPT)

Read and Answer:

Read, meditate, journal, and research the today's verses (USE YOUR FAVORITE TRANSLATION):

- Proverbs 31:1-31

Question 1: Who is Proverbs 31 for?

Week 1: Perception

DAY 2

Read and Answer:

Read, meditate, journal, and research today's verses (USE YOUR FAVORITE TRANSLATION):

- Proverbs 31:1-31.

Question 2: What is your perception of Proverbs 31?

Week 1: Perception

❧

DAY 3

WEEKLY VIDEO: HTTPS://YOUTU.BE/Y-GAG9IPMVQ

One thing to understand is that Proverbs 31 was inspired by God to a mother, who shared this wisdom with her son, King Lemuel, who then wrote it down. There are two ways to view this chapter. One way is in the context of a strong wife and where her strength comes from. The second way is as an allegory of the Bride of Christ, the New Testament Church. We can see New Testament revelation in Old Testament writings. Proverbs 31 is for men and women because we are all part of the Bride of Christ!

God created man and then made him a helper, a woman, from Adam's side. The Bride of Christ was meant to work together as a team to bring God's Kingdom, Heaven, to Earth. Even though we all are a team, we have different gifts and talents, and our identities are in Christ, not each other. We are to affirm and encourage each other. We are a complete person in Jesus Christ.

*In 2016, I had to have surgery to remove my fallopian tubes. A while after surgery, I started feeling incomplete as a woman and asked my husband if he saw me differently. I knew this was a silly question because I knew his answer. He assured me that, of course, he didn't see me any differently. My husband saw me how Christ does: by my true identity in Christ. **The amazing thing at this time was that my husband and I didn't understand our identities in Christ.***

God is always working and teaching even when we are unaware. Your past and scars are NOT your identity. They are just part of your story to help guide you in your journey of the Kingdom life on Earth. You are the Bride of Christ! You are the Proverbs 31 woman!

Week 1: Perception

DAY 4

Action Step:

Read Proverbs 31:1-31 again. What is your perception now?

Your perceived preconception can shape your view and understanding of Scripture, which is why we are reading and rereading the chapters and verses throughout this study. This renews our minds (ROMANS 12:2), so our perception of ourselves and others changes. As you renew your mind, you will see yourself and others as Christ sees us.

Prayer Tip:

Pray for an open heart and mind as you go through this course and the strength to keep pressing in and being vulnerable in the uncomfortable moments. This is a time of healing and growth.

Week 1: Perception

¹ King Lemuel's royal words of wisdom:
These are the inspired words my mother taught me.
² Listen, my dear son, son of my womb.
You are the answer to my prayers, my son.
³ So keep yourself sexually pure
from the promiscuous, wayward woman.
Don't waste the strength of your anointing
on those who ruin kings—
you'll live to regret it!
⁴ For you are a king, Lemuel,
and it's never fitting for a king to be drunk on wine
or for rulers to crave alcohol.
⁵ For when they drink they forget justice
and ignore the rights of those in need,
those who depend on them for leadership.
⁶⁻⁷ Strong drink is given to the terminally ill,
who are suffering at the brink of death.
Wine is for those in depression
in order to drown their sorrows.
Let them drink and forget their poverty and misery.

> *⁸ But you are to be a king who speaks up on behalf*
> *of the disenfranchised*
> *and pleads for the legal rights of the defenseless*
> *and those who are dying.*
> *⁹ Be a righteous king, judging on behalf of the poor*
> *and interceding for those most in need.* (PROVERBS
> *31:1-9, TPT)*

Weekly Highlights:

Proverbs 31 is for everyone, not just women!

Verses 1-9 are about the husband and his behaviors. The husband is mentioned several times along with their children, servants, and household. This entire chapter is written from a mother's perspective. When Scripture is designated only for certain people, others can lose out on what God wants to reveal.

Week 1: Perception

DAYS 6 AND 7

Rest and Reflect:

1. Take today and tomorrow to rest, reflect, and review everything you have experienced and learned this week.

2. Spend time with God, talk to Him, and listen.

3. Make sure you apply the action step and prayer tip.

4. Journal about anything you experience.

Week 2: Focus

DAY 1

¹⁰ Who could ever find a wife like this one —
she is a woman of strength and mighty valor!
She's full of wealth and wisdom.
The price paid for her was greater than many jewels.
¹¹ Her husband has entrusted his heart to her,
for she brings him the rich spoils of victory.
¹² All throughout her life she brings him what is good and not
    evil.
¹³ She searches out continually to possess
that which is pure and righteous.
She delights in the work of her hands.
¹⁴ She gives out revelation-truth to feed others.
She is like a trading ship bringing divine supplies
from the merchant.
¹⁵ Even in the night season she arises and sets food on the table
for hungry ones in her house and for others.
¹⁶ She sets her heart upon a field and takes it as her own.
She labors there to plant the living vines.
¹⁷ She wraps herself in strength, might, and power in all her
    works.

[18] *She tastes and experiences a better substance,*
and her shining light will not be extinguished,
no matter how dark the night.
[19] *She stretches out her hands to help the needy*
and she lays hold of the wheels of government.
[20] *She is known by her extravagant generosity to the poor,*
for she always reaches out her hands to those in need.
[21] *She is not afraid of tribulation,*
for all her household is covered in the dual garments
of righteousness and grace.
[22] *Her clothing is beautifully knit together —*
a purple gown of exquisite linen.
[23] *Her husband is famous and admired by all,*
sitting as the venerable judge of his people.
[24] *Even her works of righteousness*
she does for the benefit of her enemies.
[25] *Bold power and glorious majesty are wrapped around her*
as she laughs with joy over the latter days.
[26] *Her teachings are filled with wisdom and kindness*
as loving instruction pours from her lips.
[27] *She watches over the ways of her household*
and meets every need they have.
[28] *Her sons and daughters arise in one accord to extol her*
virtues,
and her husband arises to speak of her in glowing terms.
[29] *"There are many valiant and noble ones,*
but you have ascended above them all!"
[30] *Charm can be misleading,*
and beauty is vain and so quickly fades,
but this virtuous woman lives in the wonder, awe,
and fear of the Lord.
She will be praised throughout eternity.
[31] *So go ahead and give her the credit that is due,*
for she has become a radiant woman,

and all her loving works of righteousness deserve to be
  admired
at the gateways of every city! (PROVERBS *31:10-31,* TPT)

Read and Answer:

Read, meditate, journal, and research today's verses (USE YOUR FAVORITE TRANSLATION):

- Proverbs 31:10-31
- Galatians 4:6-7; 6:4-6
- Ephesians 4:11

Question 1: What is your focus on?

Question 2: Who are you wanting to be like? Why?

Week 2: Focus

DAY 2

Read and Answer:

Read, meditate, journal, and research today's verses (USE YOUR FAVORITE TRANSLATION):

- Proverbs 31:10-31
- Galatians 4:6-7; 6:4-6
- Ephesians 4: 11

Question 1: What are your talents? Write them down.

Question 2: How can you focus more on your talents in daily life?

Week 2: Focus

∾

DAY 3

WEEKLY VIDEO: HTTPS://YOUTU.BE/WRMG_VHAQXY

This week, we are still viewing all of Proverbs 31. Next week, we will start looking into specific verses.

"I want to be like the Proverbs 31 woman!" Have you ever said or heard this sentiment? I know I have, and it wasn't until I researched and sought God's understanding of her that I realized I didn't want to be like her! I AM HER!! (SEE GALATIANS 6:4-6) When first reading about her, I thought she was so accomplished; *what have I done compared to her?* I didn't realize she is an example of the New Testament 5-fold ministry mentioned in Ephesians 4:11. We all have different gifts and talents that we bring to the table in a way no one else can. A Proverbs 31 Woman knows she is unique, JUST LIKE YOU!

Back in October of 2007, I bought my wedding dress for our marriage in May of 2008. Well, we became pregnant in December 2007, so needless to say, the dress would not fit. Thank God for my husband's talented grandma! She was able to completely take my dress apart, shorten the length, and use the fabric to fix my dress. The dress looked just like it did when I bought it: absolutely beautiful!! Oh, by the way, his grandma doesn't read or write. God blessed her with this special gift of sewing!

I say all that to say God uses who you are. He didn't create you to be like the Proverbs 31 woman; YOU ARE HER! He made you to be His unique representation of His love on Earth, shining brightly. The church has many members who work together as the Body and the Bride of Christ. You will become what you focus on. Proverbs 31 gives an example of choosing how and what to focus on.

Week 2: Focus

DAY 4

Action Step:

Read *2 Corinthians 11:2 and Ephesians 4:11-16*. You are simultaneously the Body and the Bride of Christ! God created you to be you: His perfect Bride! He loves you, knows you, and sees the true you. God doesn't compare you to others. Take time this week to seek God and ask Him to reveal any area you need to refocus.

Prayer Tip:

1. Take time to pray regarding your talents.

2. If you are unsure what they are, ask God to show you clearly.

3. Ask how to partner with Him to best use your talents for the Kingdom.

Week 2: Focus

DAY 5

Weekly Highlights:

The Proverbs 31 woman was focused on the task at hand. She was not trying to be someone else or do their job. She knew what she was good at and kept bettering herself.

Week 2: Focus

~~~

DAYS 6 AND 7

Rest and Reflect:

1. Take today and tomorrow to rest, reflect, and review all you have experienced and learned this week.

2. Spend time with God, talk to Him, and listen.

3. Make sure you apply the action step and prayer tip.

4. Journal about anything you experience.

Week 3: Focus

DAY 1

[10] Who could ever find a wife like this one —
she is a woman of strength and mighty valor!
She's full of wealth and wisdom.
The price paid for her was greater than many jewels.
[11] Her husband has entrusted his heart to her,
for she brings him the rich spoils of victory.
[12] All throughout her life she brings him what is good and not
*   evil.* (PROVERBS 31:10-12, TPT)

Read and Answer:

Read, meditate, journal, and research todays verses (USE YOUR FAVORITE TRANSLATION):

- Proverbs 31:10-12

Question 1: How do you value yourself?

Question 2: How are you investing in yourself to grow where God calls you?

Week 3: Focus

DAY 2

10 Who could ever find a wife like this one —
she is a woman of strength and mighty valor!
She's full of wealth and wisdom.
The price paid for her was greater than many jewels.
11 Her husband has entrusted his heart to her,
for she brings him the rich spoils of victory.
12 All throughout her life she brings him what is good and not
evil. (PROVERBS 31:10-12, TPT)

Read and Answer:

Read, meditate, journal, and research todays verses (USE YOUR
FAVORITE TRANSLATION):

- Proverbs 31:10-12

Question 1: What do you believe about yourself?

Question 2: How and what are you multiplying?

Week 3: Focus

DAY 3

WEEKLY VIDEO: HTTPS://YOUTU.BE/XWZOTGVTFU8

I have defined the meaning of the word virtuous in verse 10 of Proverbs 31 as strength, efficiency, and wealth. It also means valor, integrity, and might, like an army. These additional meanings give further insight into the Proverbs 31 woman's value and how precious she is. Your value is worth more than rubies because Jesus, the Bridegroom, has covered you. Your worth and value surpass all the treasures of this world. You must embrace your value and worth to share it with the world. When you learn to value yourself, it is easier to see that you are also valued by others.

Verses 11-12 highlight her value and how she multiplies what's been given her. The Passion Translation says, *"Her husband has entrusted his heart to her... ."* The comment in its footnote says, *"has great confidence in her."* Men and women were created to be partners to multiply and subdue the Earth (GENESIS 1:28, 2:18-24) like we are partners with

45

Christ. (1 CORINTHIANS 1: 4-9) A woman can multiply everything given to her by her husband. For example, he brings her food, and she gives him a meal; he gives her his seed, and she gives him children. Everything God gives His Bride, we can multiply and use in spreading His Good News!

ˎ

Week 3: Focus

DAY 4

Action Step:

1. Take time this week to reflect on your value and walk confidently in it.

2. Make time to invest in yourself.

3. Reflect on things that you have multiplied. It can be anything — from an encouraging word you shared with others or memorizing a Bible verse to a delicious meal made and enjoyed!

Prayer Tip: Seek God this week on how He sees your value. Also, ask Him what He has for you to multiply in this season.

Week 3: Focus

DAY 5

Weekly Highlights:

Value and multiplication go hand in hand. It is hard to see what you have multiplied when you don't see your value. What we focus on becomes our reality. The Proverbs 31 woman focuses on life abundantly and lives an abundant life!

Week 3: Focus

$\sim$

DAYS 6 AND 7

Rest and Reflect:

1. Take today and tomorrow to rest, reflect, and review all you have experienced and learned this week.

2. Spend time with God, talk to Him, and listen.

3. Make sure you apply the action step and prayer tip.

4. Journal about anything you experience.

Week 4: Value and Investment

◦───∞───◦

DAY 1

¹³ She searches out continually to possess
that which is pure and righteous.
She delights in the work of her hands.
¹⁴ She gives out revelation-truth to feed others.
She is like a trading ship bringing divine supplies
from the merchant.
¹⁵ Even in the night season she arises and sets food on the
table. (PROVERBS 31:13-15, TPT)

Read and Answer:

Read, meditate, journal, and research today's verses (USE YOUR FAVORITE TRANSLATION):

- Proverbs 31:13-15
- Ephesians 4:11

Question 1: What work do you delight in?

Week 4: Value and Investment

꒰꒱

DAY 2

*¹³ She searches out continually to possess
that which is pure and righteous.
She delights in the work of her hands.
¹⁴ She gives out revelation-truth to feed others.
She is like a trading ship bringing divine supplies
from the merchant.
¹⁵ Even in the night season she arises and sets food on the
table.* (PROVERBS 31:13-15, TPT)

Read and Answer:

Read, meditate, journal, and research today's verses (USE YOUR
FAVORITE TRANSLATION):

- Proverbs 31:13-15
- Ephesians 4:11

Question 1: What do you bring to the table?

Week 4: Value and Investment

∽

DAY 3

WEEKLY VIDEO: HTTP://YOUTU.BE/8FCNEJWANZM

In verse 13, the Proverbs 31 woman is dutiful and enjoys working. She is helping others find and walk out their ministries. She knows the truth of her identity and is walking out Kingdom in all she does. She encourages, enables, exalts, and edifies those around her to step into their 5-fold ministry.

While creating this study, my husband reminded me that I encourage and help others to step into their God-given gifts and ministries. I do this no matter where God calls them. At the time he said this, I didn't really think of these as encouraging, but in reality, they were. Even when God calls people to move away, I want them to fulfill their calling, and I am truly happy for them. In this process, I also am learning more about myself and my calling.

The Proverbs 31 woman feeds others with the revelational truth she has received. This is her delight, what brings her joy. She helps, teaches, and loves all those around her.

Week 4: Value and Investment

DAY 4

Action Step:

Look up who God says you are (your truths). Examples: I am as He is (1 JOHN 4:17), I am Chosen (JOHN 15:16), and I am Loved (1 JOHN 4:9-10). Start proclaiming these truths over yourself today!

Prayer Tip:

As you pray this week, ask God to help you always see yourself as He sees you. God always sees the *you* that He created you to be!

Week 4: Value and Investment

∞

DAY 5

Weekly Highlights:

God loves what you love. He wants you to enjoy what you like because He gave you the gift for what you love.

Embrace and grow in your gifts and talents!

Week 4: Value and Investment

❦

Rest and Reflect:

1. Take today and tomorrow to rest, reflect, and review all you have experienced and learned this week.

2. Spend time with God, talk to Him, and listen.

3. Make sure you apply the action step and prayer tip.

4. Journal about anything you experience.

Week 5: Strength and Season

⤜⤛

DAY 1

16 She sets her heart upon a field and takes it as her own.
She labors there to plant the living vines.
17 She wraps herself in strength, might, and power in all her
*   works. (PROVERBS 31:16-17, TPT)*

Read and Answer:

Read, meditate, journal, and research today's verses (USE YOUR
FAVORITE TRANSLATION):

- Proverbs 31:16-17
- John 14:12

Question 1: Where does your strength come from? (FIND IT IN
SCRIPTURE)

Week 5: Strength and Season

^{16} She sets her heart upon a field and takes it as her own. She labors there to plant the living vines.
^{17} She wraps herself in strength, might, and power in all her works. (PROVERBS 31:16-17, TPT)

Read and Answer:

Read, meditate, journal, and research today's verses (USE YOUR FAVORITE TRANSLATION):

- Proverbs 31:16-17
- John 14:12

Question 2: Are you in a planting season or a growing season?

Week 5: Strength and Season

❧⤳⤻

DAY 3

WEEKLY VIDEO: HTTPS://YOUTU.BE/MERVS0QC1RC

In verse 16, the Proverbs 31 woman has her heart set on where she needs to be during the season of life she is in. She carefully considers and buys a field. Each of us goes through seasons unique to our growth and understanding. She now has good soil (foundation) for planting. You are good soil because you were chosen in Christ before the foundation of the world. (EPHESIANS 1:4) Learning to know the need for rest in each season is essential.

It takes as much strength if not more, to rest in the season of growth as it does in the planting season. The planting season is labor intensive, whereas the growing season is patiently waiting. God is working in the background where we can't see; we can only trust. You are naturally a Kingdom woman who has only to rise from the dirt and ashes of the past.

In our garden, every year, we burn our Christmas tree because the ash is good for the soil. Before we planted our red raspberry patch, we burned a brush pile. By doing this step, the seeds planted in the dirt and ashes became our garden and berry patch, and both yielded a greater harvest!

You are anointed with power to do the works of Jesus and even greater works! (JOHN 14:12) You are destined for more!

Week 5: Strength and Season

❧

Action Step:

Be creative! Write or draw a blueprint of how you can embrace this to reach your goals. Small, manageable steps are good. They allow you to digest, absorb, and rejoice as you complete them.

Prayer Tip:

Ask God how to partner with Him this season to reach your goals. Ask Him to guide your steps and trust His leading no matter what.

Week 5: Strength and Season

~~~~~~

DAY 5

Weekly Highlights:

Our physical strength plays a vital role in our lives, but it is our spiritual strength that what will carry us through the tough times. Another aspect of our strength is knowing when to exercise (invest) and when to rest.

Week 5: Strength and Seasons

⤜⤛⤜⤛

DAYS 6 AND 7

Rest and Reflect:

1. Take today and tomorrow to rest, reflect, and review all you have experienced and learned this week.

2. Spend time with God, talk to Him, and listen.

3. Make sure you apply the action step and prayer tip.

4. Journal about anything you experience.

Week 6: Shine Through

〜

DAY 1

18 She tastes and experiences a better substance,
and her shining light will not be extinguished,
no matter how dark the night.
19 She stretches out her hands to help the needy
and she lays hold of the wheels of government.
20 She is known by her extravagant generosity to the poor,
   (PROVERBS 31:18-20, TPT)

Read and Answer:

Read, meditate, journal, and research today's verses (USE YOUR
FAVORITE TRANSLATION):

- Proverbs 31:18-20

Question 1: How has God brought you through your past, causing
you to shine?

Week 6: Shine Through

DAY 2

18 She tastes and experiences a better substance,
and her shining light will not be extinguished,
no matter how dark the night.
19 She stretches out her hands to help the needy
and she lays hold of the wheels of government.
20 She is known by her extravagant generosity to the poor,
(PROVERBS *31:18-20,* TPT)

Read and Answer:

Read, meditate, journal, and research today's verses (USE YOUR
FAVORITE TRANSLATION):

- Proverbs 31:18-20

Question 1: Have you put your past under your feet? Why or
why not?

Week 6: Shine Through

DAY 3

WEEKLY VIDEO: HTTPS://YOUTU.BE/VDBYN0PU7AO

Verse 18 talks about how she has good or better. To admit that she has good things, she had to let go of what wasn't good. The verse continues with how she is a shining light that can't be put out. She has not allowed circumstances to hold her back. Jesus is your hope, not your circumstance. Now is the time to let the past go and let your light shine.

Those things that have held you back no longer define you or your future. Those experiences no longer have power over you. They are just part of your testimony, which will help set others free! Your testimony is someone else's prophecy.

When writing this study my husband and I had been married for 14 years and together for 15 years. For nearly 13 years of our marriage, we had lived with his parents off and on. We had prayed and tried in our own power to get our own place several times. We had finally gotten to the point where we were giving up trying. Then, at the end of 2019, on New Year's Eve day, we signed the papers to order our new home. By May of 2020, we moved into our new home on Mother's Day!

In 2021, I had been talking to our friends who were in the same position we were in at the beginning of our marriage. The Lord led me to share our testimony with them and prophesy their new home over them. Later that year, the home they hoped to buy fell through. We didn't lose hope; we put our faith in God, who provides! They received a better one before the end of the year!

Week 6: Shine Through

DAY 4

Action Step:

Share your testimony with someone you trust, or write it out in your journal and date it. Journaling can be helpful in letting things go and is an excellent way to see your growth.

I wrote letters to God when angry, sad, and confused. I also have thanked Him but need to write more letters of joy and thanksgiving.

Prayer Tip:

As you let go of the past, ask God to fill those spaces of your heart with His ever-increasing love, wisdom, and strength.

Week 6: Shine Through

DAY 5

Weekly Highlights:

What you have and carry is good; do not let the circumstances of this world cover your shining light. You are a blessing to everyone you meet!

We don't always get to see our impact on others, and that's okay. Planting seeds is just as important as harvesting the fruit.

Week 6: Shine Through

DAYS 6 AND 7

Rest and Reflect:

1. Take today and tomorrow to rest, reflect, and review all you have experienced and learned this week.

2. Spend time with God, talk to Him, and listen.

3. Make sure you apply the action step and prayer tip.

4. Journal about anything you experience.

Week 7: Covering

DAY 1

21 She is not afraid of tribulation,
for all her household is covered in the dual garments
of righteousness and grace.
22 Her clothing is beautifully knit together —
a purple gown of exquisite linen. (PROVERBS 31:21-22, TPT)

Read and Answer:

Read, meditate, journal, and research today's verses (USE YOUR FAVORITE TRANSLATION):

- Proverbs 31:21-22
- Joshua 2
- 1 Peter 2:9

Question 1: What is your covering?

Week 7: Covering

DAY 2

21 She is not afraid of tribulation,
for all her household is covered in the dual garments
of righteousness and grace.
22 Her clothing is beautifully knit together —
a purple gown of exquisite linen. (PROVERBS *31:21-22,* TPT)

Read and Answer:

Read, meditate, journal, and research today's verses (USE YOUR FAVORITE TRANSLATION):

- Proverbs 31:21-22
- Joshua 2
- 1 Peter 2:9

Question 1: What is your covering and how is it made?

103

Question 2: What does your covering mean to you?

Week 7: Covering

DAY 3

WEEKLY VIDEO: HTTP://YOUTU.BE/S92FGUGDR24

I was really struggling with writing and conveying my thoughts the way I wanted to for the notes in this week's session. My notes and thoughts didn't seem to sync together. Then, one of our girls asked me if I could fix her stuffed animal's leg. I said that I would sew it for her. After finishing, God gave me the thought that this is how things are brought together — one stitch at a time. There is no rush. Bring what you have, and He will sew it together into a beautiful masterpiece!

Today's verses from Proverbs are focused on clothing and how it covers not only the woman but also her household. She has no need to fear seasons of hardship; they are all covered by God.

This reminds me of Rahab in Joshua 2. She covered the spies and then trusted them to spare her and her household, even though she and her family were not Israelites. By this faith and trust, Rahab and her family were not only spared — Rahab is in the lineage of Jesus Christ! She was the mother of Boaz, who married Ruth (the Moabite). Rahab, her family, and Ruth were all covered by God, which proves He loves and chooses all!

We must choose to partner with Him! God knits us all together, covering our mistakes with righteousness and grace. We become the body of Christ dressed in purple, a sign of royalty. You are a Royal Priesthood! (1 PETER 2:9)

Week 7: Covering

DAY 4

Action Step:

This week, research the meaning of covering (clothing) in the two verses from Proverbs and cross-reference them with other verses. Then, reread the above Scripture references and write down the revelation you receive.

Prayer Tip:

Before diving into the action step, pray and ask God to open your heart and eyes to what He wants to reveal to you.

Week 7: Covering

DAY 5

Weekly Highlights:

You are covered by Jesus Christ! You are a beautiful tapestry sewn together with care and beautifully stitched.

Each step you take is a new stitch, pulling you closer to Him.

Week 7: Covering

DAYS 6 AND 7

Rest and Reflect:

1. Take today and tomorrow to rest, reflect, and review all you have experienced and learned this week.

2. Spend time with God, talk to Him, and listen.

3. Make sure you apply the action step and prayer tip.

4. Journal about anything you experience.

Week 8: Honor and Vision

²³ Her husband is famous and admired by all,
sitting as the venerable judge of his people.
²⁴ Even her works of righteousness
she does for the benefit of her enemies.
²⁵ Bold power and glorious majesty are wrapped around her
as she laughs with joy over the latter days. (PROVERBS
31:23-25, TPT)

Read and Answer:

Read, meditate, journal, and research today's verses (USE YOUR FAVORITE TRANSLATION):

- Proverbs 31:23-25
- Proverbs 4:24-27
- Matthew 10:41-42
- Habakkuk 2:2

Question 1: How are you honoring those around you?

Week 8: Honor and Vision

⌒⌒⌒

DAY 2

²³ *Her husband is famous and admired by all,*
sitting as the venerable judge of his people.
²⁴ *Even her works of righteousness*
she does for the benefit of her enemies.
²⁵ *Bold power and glorious majesty are wrapped around her*
as she laughs with joy over the latter days. (PROVERBS
   31:23-25, TPT)

Read and Answer:

Read, meditate, journal, and research today's verses (USE YOUR FAVORITE TRANSLATION):

- Proverbs 31:23-25
- Proverbs 4:24-27
- Matthew 10:41-42
- Habakkuk 2:2

Question 1: What is your vision?

Question 2: Where are you looking?

Week 8: Honor and Vision

DAY 3

WEEKLY VIDEO: HTTPS://YOUTU.BE/BAmL_0GB7DM

The Proverbs 31 woman's marriage serves as an example to the people. As we read in verse 23, her husband is famous and admired at the city gates. He is honored and is a respected judge in his community. Verse 24 says that she does righteous works for her enemies. In the footnote of The Passion Translation for this verse, enemies were most likely Canaanites, and the relations between them and the Hebrews were much like the Jews and Samaritans. She chose to rise above and help those that hurt her. (JAMES 5:16)

We've all been hurt by the pain and sorrow we've experienced. Things come at us sometimes, and we feel like giving up, or we feel unqualified. It's in these moments we need to step out in faith.

Once, when I was struggling with stepping forward into my calling, I was encouraged by the Director of Legacy Academy of Kingdom Living to stay focused and not look away. The advice she shared was from Habakkuk 2:2 (NKJV). It says, "Then the Lord answered me and said: 'Write the vision And make it plain on tablets, That he may run who reads it.'" It was my time to run, and the result was this study.

This is your time to focus and not look to the right or the left but straight ahead. (PROVERBS 4:24-27)

Week 8: Honor and Vision

~~~~~~

DAY 4

Action Step:

Write your vision down like it says in Habakkuk 2.

Prayer Tip:

Take time this week, before writing your vision, to pray for those who have hurt you. This is a step of releasing the hurt so God can fill that area with His love.

It's also a step that will cause greater clarity as you see and write your vision.

Week 8: Honor and Vision

Weekly Highlights:

Where honor is given, it is also received. (MATTHEW 10:41-42) Honor and agreement aren't the same. You can give honor and not agree with a person. Paul disagreed with Peter's behavior but still honored him. (GALATIANS 2:11-14)

Week 8: Honor and Vision

◦⟊⟋◦

DAYS 6 AND 7

Rest and Reflect:

1. Take today and tomorrow to rest, reflect, and review all you have experienced and learned this week.

2. Spend time with God, talk to Him, and listen.

3. Make sure you apply the action step and prayer tip.

4. Journal about anything you experience.

Week 9: Study and Teaching

26 Her teachings are filled with wisdom and kindness
as loving instruction pours from her lips.
27 She watches over the ways of her household
and meets every need they have. (PROVERBS 31:26-27, TPT)

Read and Answer:

Read, meditate, journal, and research the following verses (USE YOUR FAVORITE TRANSLATION):

- Proverbs 31:26-27
- Proverbs 22:6
- Luke 5:16
- Matthew 8:23-27

Question 1: What are you studying or spending time on?

Week 9: Study and Teaching

❧❧

DAY 2

> ²⁶ Her teachings are filled with wisdom and kindness
> as loving instruction pours from her lips.
> ²⁷ She watches over the ways of her household
> and meets every need they have. (PROVERBS 31:26-27, TPT)

Read and Answer:

Read, meditate, journal, and research the following verses (USE YOUR FAVORITE TRANSLATION):

- Proverbs 31:26-27
- Proverbs 22:6
- Luke 5:16
- Matthew 8:23-27

Question 1: How do you treat yourself?

Question 2: What are you teaching others?

Week 9: Study and Teaching

⤳⤳⤳

DAY 3

WEEKLY VIDEO: HTTPS://YOUTU.BE/HIOlgpPVm5k

Verse 26 talks about the Proverbs 31 woman opening her mouth and speaking with wisdom and the law of kindness. Are we watching what comes out of our mouths? Are we proclaiming life abundantly? Our family has made it a priority to remind each other to declare Kingdom and life over each other. At times, this has been a struggle for me. A book I recommend to help with this is *Loving Your Kids On Purpose* by Danny Silk.

This topic continues into verse 27, discussing how she watches over her family. The best way to watch over and guard our family is by Kingdom Living. We teach by example. Danny Silk's book teaches how to present choices to our kids, such as *you can do the dishes, or I will do them, and you will clean the chicken coop.* By teaching our children to make good choices at a young age, we give them the wisdom to do the same as adults. (PROVERBS 22:6)

Verse 27 also mentions the Proverbs 31 woman not being idle and she meets the needs of her family. Part of meeting the needs of her family is also self-care.

It is challenging to help others when we are burned out. We must ensure that we are part of our household and care for ourselves as well. Jesus took time to be with His Father and time to rest. (LUKE 5:16 AND MATTHEW 8:23-27)

Week 9: Study and Teaching

❧

DAY 4

Action Step:

Be intentional about setting time to be with God; it can be in prayer, worship, crafting, or silence. Also, set aside some time for self-care.

My Prayer for You:

Father, I speak Your overflowing wisdom and abundant life over her. May Your clarity and vision flow in and through every area of her life in Jesus' Precious Name. Amen.

Week 9: Study and Teaching

DAY 5

Weekly Highlights:

What you study and pour yourself into is what you acquire knowledge in, and it's also what flows from you. Are we speaking love and abundant life over ourselves, family, and friends? This is how we keep guard and give wisdom to our families and all around us.

Week 9: Study and Teaching

ᏪᏪᏪ

DAYS 6 AND 7

Rest and Reflect:

1. Take today and tomorrow to rest, reflect, and review all you have experienced and learned this week.

2. Spend time with God, talk to Him, and listen.

3. Make sure you apply the action step and prayer tip.

4. Journal about anything you experience.

Week 10: Encourage

DAY 1

^{28} Her sons and daughters arise in one accord to extol her
  virtues,
and her husband arises to speak of her in glowing terms.
    (PROVERBS 31:28, TPT)

Read and Answer:

Read, meditate, journal, and research the following verses (USE YOUR FAVORITE TRANSLATION):

- Proverbs 31:28
- Romans 12:2

Question 1: How do you encourage your family or team?

Week 10: Encourage

DAY 2

> ^{28} *Her sons and daughters arise in one accord to extol her virtues,*
> *and her husband arises to speak of her in glowing terms.*
> (PROVERBS 31:28, TPT)

Read and Answer:

Read, meditate, journal, and research the following verses (USE YOUR FAVORITE TRANSLATION):

- Proverbs 31:28
- Romans 12:2

Question 1: How does your family or team encourage you?

Week 10: Encourage

DAY 3

WEEKLY VIDEO: HTTPS://YOUTU.BE/URTD3GKAISM

Every parent or team leader wants their children or team to make the right choices and grow to be the best they can be. This starts at home with how we are raising up the next generation. If the home consists of fighting, yelling, or speaking badly about others, that is what will be learned and shared. I know as adults and spouses that we don't always agree, but it's how we handle and discuss the things we don't agree about that will influence those closest to us. It can sometimes be challenging to raise children or interact with those under our leadership. There tend to be many times when we are likely to think: *what am I doing wrong?*

After our children or team members accomplish something remarkable, we applaud their achievements. Yet, how often do we follow it with a comment like, "Why don't they do this all the time?" In verse 28, it talks about how the Proverbs 31 woman's children rise up and exalt her. Her children do this because she has raised them by example and encouraged them. She doesn't lift them up and then criticize them.

Example: When someone tells you how good or sweet your children are and you reply by saying you wish they were like that all the time — instead, say thank you and share that praise with your children.

Verse 28 continues with how her husband speaks of her with praise or glowing terms. These few lines show us a family dynamic of love and praise in how parents treat each other and their children. There is a continuous following of love, honor, and respect. This is the example our kids will carry into their relationships. It's also an example of how leadership works. We raise up our children and teams to surpass us, not giving them 90% of what we have and withholding 10%. Jesus gave us 100% of Himself; we are to do the same!

Week 10: Encourage

DAY 4

Action Step:

This week, as you encourage those around you, watch for and stop signs of negativity before these cross your lips. I am working on this as well. It is a process of renewing our minds. (ROMANS 12:2)

Prayer:

Father, help me filter my thoughts and words before speaking them out and over myself and my family. Let my thoughts and words be Your thoughts and words overflowing to my family in Jesus' name. Amen

Week 10: Encourage

DAY 5

Weekly Highlights:

Having a family and leading a team are alike in many ways. You must be loving, understanding, willing to listen and learn from your family and team.

Week 10: Encourage

DAYS 6 AND 7

Rest and Reflect:

1. Take today and tomorrow to rest, reflect, and review all you have experienced and learned this week.

2. Spend time with God, talk to Him, and listen.

3. Make sure you apply the action step and prayer tip.

4. Journal about anything you experience.

Week 11: Inspire

DAY 1

[29] *"There are many valiant and noble ones,*
but you have ascended above them all!"
[30] *Charm can be misleading,*
and beauty is vain and so quickly fades,
but this virtuous woman lives in the wonder, awe,
and fear of the Lord.
She will be praised throughout eternity. (PROVERBS
31:29-30, TPT)

Read and Answer:

Read, meditate, journal, and research the following verses (USE YOUR FAVORITE TRANSLATION):

- Proverbs 31:29-30

Question 1: Name a woman who has inspired you. How has she inspired you?

Week 11: Inspire

DAY 2

> [29] *"There are many valiant and noble ones,*
> *but you have ascended above them all!"*
> [30] *Charm can be misleading,*
> *and beauty is vain and so quickly fades,*
> *but this virtuous woman lives in the wonder, awe,*
> *and fear of the Lord.*
> *She will be praised throughout eternity.* (PROVERBS
> *31:29-30*, TPT)

Read and Answer:

Read, meditate, journal, and research the following verses (USE YOUR FAVORITE TRANSLATION):

- Proverbs 31:29-30

Question 1: How do you want to influence others?

Week 11: Inspire

DAY 3

WEEKLY VIDEO: HTTPS://YOUTU.BE/RNEmME26b0k

Vulnerability moment here: I thought these two verses would be some of the easier ones to cover, but it proved to be more of a challenge than I thought. I love how God is always teaching us and showing us there is more to learn.

Verse 29 says, "Many daughters have done well, But you excel them all." (NKJV) This verse got me thinking. Initially, I thought about all the women I admired and wondered how I surpassed them. Then, I realized that I was comparing myself to them. Finally, I had this revelation — since we are ALL Proverbs 31 women, all those ladies we look up to have also excelled. Each generation of Proverbs 31 women leaves a mark through their teaching, wisdom, and revelation that they have shared with us.

In verse 30, it mentions how charm is deceitful; it is a fake "you" that you put on to fit in, and beauty is the mask you wear to get attention.

Both charm and beauty are passing, but the women who have gone before put those things under their feet. Their example taught us a loving reverence of God and encouraged us to step out in His confidence.

Week 11: Inspire

Action Step:

You have greater influence than you realize. The people you have looked up to have qualities that have encouraged you. Think of three qualities you like about yourself? Do you know God loves these things about you as well?

Prayer Tip:

Pray about how to use these qualities to better guide and encourage those around you.

Week 11: Inspire

DAY 5

Weekly Highlights:

You are excelling every day!! You are an influencer!! You inspire others!!

Week 11: Inspire

DAYS 6 AND 7

Rest and Reflect:

1. Take today and tomorrow to rest, reflect, and review all you have experienced and learned this week.

2. Spend time with God, talk to Him, and listen.

3. Make sure you apply the action step and prayer tip.

4. Journal about anything you experience.

Week 12: Arise

DAY 1

31 So go ahead and give her the credit that is due,
for she has become a radiant woman,
and all her loving works of righteousness deserve to be
admired
at the gateways of every city! (PROVERBS 31:31, TPT)

Read and Answer:

Read, meditate, journal, and research (USE YOUR FAVORITE TRANSLATION):

- Proverbs 31:31

The New King James Version says: *"Give her of the fruit of her hands, And let her own works praise her in the gates."*

Question 1: Who are you? Take a moment to reflect on how you see yourself.

Week 12: Arise

³¹ So go ahead and give her the credit that is due,
for she has become a radiant woman,
and all her loving works of righteousness deserve to be
  admired
at the gateways of every city! (PROVERBS 31:31, TPT)

Read and Answer:

Read, meditate, journal, and research (USE YOUR FAVORITE TRANSLATION):

- Proverbs 31:31

The New King James Version says: *"Give her of the fruit of her hands, And let her own works praise her in the gates."*

Question 1: What have you discovered about yourself during this study?

Question 2: How does God see you?

Week 12: Arise

DAY 3

WEEKLY VIDEO: HTTPS://YOUTU.BE/5RUA0LETZNI

The Proverbs 31 woman is honored at the gates for the love she shares. Even when the world doesn't acknowledge or honor your efforts, Jesus sees His Bride and admires you! It can be hard to not receive honor and recognition from those around you. However, the truth is that the spotlight isn't supposed to be on us. Matthew 5:16 says that when we let our light shine, and they see our good deeds, God is seen. The spotlight is to be on God. He is on display in our lives.

Jesus sees you and knows your heart. You have risen above the ashes and conquered. You are His radiant, righteous Bride clothed in white, walking with Him forevermore!

Week 12: Arise

DAY 4

Action Step:

Write down all that you have learned and overcome. Write and pray your own prayer.

Prayer:

Father thank You for Your unwavering love and strength. I speak Your continue revelation over me as I continue to grow and flourish as the Proverbs 31 woman I am in Jesus name. Amen

Week 12: Arise

DAY 5

Weekly Highlights:

You are worthy of praise! You have worked hard, and it is appreciated!! God loves you, your passion, and the work you are doing for the Kingdom!!

Week 12: Arise

DAYS 6 AND 7

Rest and Reflect:

1. Take today and tomorrow to rest, reflect, and review all you have experienced and learned this week.

2. Spend time with God, talk to Him, and listen.

3. Make sure you apply the action step and prayer tip.

4. Journal about anything you experience.

Follow Us...

Website:

https://www.oneheartliving.com

Facebook:

One Heart Living Page: https://www.facebook.com/
OneHeartLiving

Proverbs 31 Woman Group https://www.facebook.com/
groups/1015558252444325

Instagram:

https://www.instagram.com/oneheartliving/

About the Author

Amanda Stoneman is a biblical life coach, author, and ministry leader. She lives in Ohio on their family's ranch with her husband, Brian, and their three beautiful girls.

Proverbs 31 Woman: A Twelve Week Study Guide is her first book. She continues to write using her life experiences and revelations to help others!

Made in the USA
Columbia, SC
15 April 2025